A
Basic
Grammar
Dictionary
for
Anyone

D1417169

George Ann Gregory, Ph.D.

Published by *MJG Publishing,* 7012 Petit Avenue, Lake Balboa, CA 91406

Manufactured in the United States of America.

ISBN 0-9704060-0-2

Fifth Printing

OTHER PUBLISHED WORKS

BY

GEORGE ANN GREGORY

American English Punctuation for Anyone

> A Punctuation Guide written for high school and college students, English Language Learners, teachers, business people, writers, and editors.

American English Composition for Anyone

> A composition workbook written for high school and college students, English Language Learners, teachers, business people, writers, and editors.

Grammar Works for Better Writing

> Series Developer and Coordinator

> A series of workbooks and teacher manuals that teach grammar to students in grades 3 through 9.

ABOUT THE AUTHOR

George Ann Gregory has a Ph.D. in Applied Linguistics. She is a lifelong educator who has developed language and literacy with ages preschool through adults.

She has worked with a variety of ethnic and linguistic groups, including Amerindian, Southeast Asian, Latin American, Middle-Eastern, European, African American, Hispanic American, and Anglo American.

Her research includes grammatical analysis of compositions and teaching methods that work. Her publications include research articles, essays, short stories, poetry, and children's stories and texts.

CONTENTS

Introduction

This book contains a list of the most frequently encountered grammatical terms. Entries are organized in alphabetical order. The example for each grammar term precedes the definition itself. Look at the following example of interrogative pronoun to see this pattern.

Interrogative Pronoun

To *whom* do you wish to speak? *Whose* shoe is this?
interrogative pronoun   interrogative pronoun

Interrogative pronouns begin with *wh-*. You use them to make questions. The interrogative pronouns are *what, who, which, whose,* and *whom*. **See also *pronoun.***

Many entries have "see also" noted at the end of the definition. You can refer to these additional entries when more information is needed.

The charts in the back of the book provide additional information about certain grammar terms.

COMMON TYPES OF GRAMMARS

There are many different approaches to grammar. We've included a brief description of the four most common. Definitions have been included from traditional and other grammars.

CASE

In case grammar, the verb is the most important part of the sentence. The verb has relationships in meaning with the words surrounding it.

The man *shot* the deer with a crossbow.

There is a relationship in meaning between *shot* and *crossbow*. Since the crossbow is the instrument for shooting, it is in the instrumental case. (For more information, read

Fillmore 1968.)

DESCRIPTIVE

Descriptive grammar describes how people really use language. It does not say what is right or wrong.

Generative Transformational

Noam Chomsky proposed this theory in 1967. This grammar tries to provide a model to describe all languages. His studies tried to capture all the rules speakers use to produce language. (For more information, read Chomsky 1965.)

Traditional

Traditional grammar is usually based on the rules for Latin and Greek. Many of these rules do not exist in English. When applied to English, they often cause confusion. Most school grammar books teach traditional grammar.

ABSOLUTE PHRASE

My hands shaking with excitement, I opened my presents.
  <small>absolute phrase</small>

An absolute phrase has a noun or noun phrase plus a participle.
In the above absolute
phrase, the noun is
hands and the participle

> An absolute phrase adds spice to the sentence
> *I opened my presents.*

is *shaking.* Use an absolute phrase to provide more description,
vary a sentence, or change the meaning of a sentence. **See also**
noun phrase, participle, **and** *modifier.*

ABSTRACT NOUN

It was hard to get her *agreement.*
  <small>abstract noun</small>

His *bravery* was admired by all who knew him.
  <small>abstract noun</small>

Her *thoughts* were private.
  <small>abstract noun</small>

An abstract noun names a concept or idea. **See also** *concrete
noun* **and** *noun.*

ACTIVE VOICE

The dog *bit* the cow.   Sarah *hit* the ball.
  <small>subject   verb</small>   <small>subject verb</small>

A verb is in active voice when the subject does the action named
by the verb. **See also** *voice.*

ACTION VERB

Jeremy *runs* down the hill.

action verb

Woody *ate* too much cherry pie.

action verb

The dog *terrified* the children.

action verb

An action verb appears in the predicate of a sentence. It shows the action. **See also *linking verb, stative verb, verb subject, predicate, predicate adjective,* and *predicate noun.***

ADJECTIVE

The *blue* sky made the day look *hot*.

adjective noun   noun   adjective

The *seven* dwarfs worked in an *old* mine.

adjective noun   adjective noun

The tiny, green balloon floated into the sky.

adjective adjective noun

Use an adjective to tell more about a noun. An adjective usually tells how many, what kind, what color or size, or which one. Adjectives often come just before the noun. **See also *noun.***

ADJECTIVE CLAUSE

My mother, *who is eighty years old,* still teaches school.
Non-defining adjective clause

Adam chose the shoe *that had the best arch support.*
defining adjective clause

An adjective clause is a part of a sentence, but it has its own subject and verb. An adjective clause usually begins with a relative pronoun, a word relating or connecting the adjective clause to a word or phrase coming before it. (In the above examples, the relative pronouns are *who* and *that.*)

Use an adjective clause when that is the clearest way to express your idea. It allows you to put more information in each sentence.

See also *clause, pronoun,* **and** *subordinator.*

ADJECTIVE PHRASE

The Scout troop took a *very slow* train through Tibet.
adjective phrase

A phrase is a group of words working as a unit. An adjective phrase has an adjective or an adjective plus its modifiers. It provides more information about a noun or noun phrase.

ADJECTIVE PRONOUNS

Hand me *those* books.   Carol would like *her* coat.
adjective pronoun   **adjective pronoun**

An adjective pronoun is a pronoun used as an adjective. **See also** *adjective, demonstrative pronouns, possessive pronouns,* **and** *pronouns.*

ADVERB

She sang *beautifully*.
    verb   adverb

Suddenly, he jumped up.
    adverb with a sentence

She dances *less* gracefully than the others.
    adverb   adverb

The class liked his *extremely* bright tie.
    adverb   adjective

An adverb tells more about a sentence, a verb, an adjective, or sometimes another adverb. An adverb changes the quality of the word or sentence it tells more about. It tells where, when, how, or how often. **See also *verb, adjective,* and *sentence.***

ADVERBIAL

Even though he loved to eat, he was late to dinner.
    adverbial clause

The telephone rang just *as we started the meal.*
    adverbial clause

She ran *swiftly and gracefully* through the grass.
    adverbial phrase

The child wept *pitifully* over her lost doll.
    single word adverbial

An adverbial is a word, phrase, or clause acting like an adverb. **See also *adverb, clause, main clause,* and *phrase.***

ADVERBIAL CLAUSE

Even though he loved to eat, he was late to dinner.
adverbial

An adverbial clause acts like an adverb and modifies a main clause. **See also *adverb, clause, main clause,* and *phrase.***

ADVERBIAL PHRASE

She ran *swiftly and gracefully* through the grass.
adverbial compound phrase

She ran *with great speed.*
adverbial prepositional phrase

An adverbial phrase acts like an adverb. It tells where, when, and how. **See also *adverb and phrase.***

AGREEMENT

There are two kinds of agreement in English grammar.

The Cocker Spaniel **jumps** for joy.
singular subject   singular verb

> A singular subject must have a verb in the singular form.

The children **play** at the park.
plural subject   plural verb

> A plural subject must have a verb in the plural form.

The subject and verb must have agreement.

AGREEMENT *(Continued)*

English has the remnants of an older verb system. In this system, the verb took a different ending for each person. See *Person.* Today, the only change is for third person singular. This includes the pronouns *he, she,* and *it.* These verbs take an "s" ending. **See also *subject, verb, singular, and plural.***

> *Robert* is coming to the party. *He* is bringing a pizza.
> antecedent   pronoun

> *Kerensa* called to say *she* will be late.
> antecedent   pronoun

> *Sam and Sara* said *they* can't come.
>   antecedent   pronoun

The pronoun and its antecedent agree in number—singular or

Gender
Male: *he, his, him* Female: *she, her, hers*

plural—and gender—masculine, feminine, or neutral. **See also *antecedent, gender, plural, pronoun,* and *singular.***

ANTECEDENT

> *Carrie,* can *you* name the fifty states?
> antecedent   pronoun

When a pronoun refers or directs your attention back to a noun, the noun is its antecedent.

> *The boy* who has the dog said hello.
>
>   antecedent   adjective clause

When an adjective clause comes right after a noun that it describes, that noun is its antecedent.

In general, the word *antecedent* means something coming before: *ante* means *before.* In grammar, we use the word to show the same idea. **See also *pronoun, noun,* and *adjective clause.***

APPOSITIVE

Mr. Shea, *my scuba teacher*, has been diving for years.

noun   appositive

Use an appositive to give more information about a noun or noun phrase. An appositive is a noun or noun phrase that identifies another noun, noun phrase, or pronoun. **See also *noun* and *noun phrase*.**

> *My scuba teacher* is a noun phrase. It is also an appositive because it identifies the noun, *Mr. Shea.*

ARTICLE

I would like *a* sandwich, please.

      article

I just saw *a* squirrel.

      article

> Use *a* before singular nouns beginning with a consonant sound to mean one kind of person, place, thing, or idea.

It is *an* hour until we go to the beach.

      article

Here's *an* apple for your lunch.

      article

> Use *an* before singular nouns beginning with a vowel sound to mean one kind of person, place, thing, or idea.

Hand me *the* books from my desk.

      article

I like *the* cat over there.

      article

> Use *the* for plural nouns or to show a particular or definite thing, person, or place.

There are only three articles in the English language: *a*, *an*, and *the*. They always come before a noun, noun phrase, or words used as nouns. **See also *noun* and *noun phrase*.**

Auxiliary (Helping) verb

There are three different ways to use an auxiliary verb.

Creating Tense

Grandmother *will* leave tomorrow.

auxiliary verb

Creating Mood

Our math teacher *may* give us a test today.

auxiliary verb

Creating Voice

The football game *was* played on Saturday.

auxiliary verb

You add an auxiliary or helping verb to the base form of a verb or participle to make more tenses and to show mood or voice. Auxiliary means giving assistance or help. Some auxiliary verbs are *have, may, can, must,* and *will.* **See the Modal Auxiliary Verb chart in the Appendix for a more complete understanding. See also** *verb, base form, tense, mood, participle,* **and** *voice.*

BASE FORM

Base Form	Other Forms	
help	helpful	helpfully
run	ran	will run
think	thinks	thought
be	am	was
walk	walking	walked
fruit	fruitful	fruitfully
provide	proves	provider
secure	secures	securely

A base form of a word is its root word or form. You can make other forms of the word from this.

BE VERB

Be As a Copula

Margarita *was* a school teacher.
noun phrase

I *am* handsome.   The oak tree *is* in the pasture.
adjective phrase   prepositional phrase

Be is the primary copula in English. *Be* as a copula may be followed by a noun phrase, an adjective phrase, or a prepositional phrase. The copula links the subject to one of these kinds of phrases. The copula is a *linking verb*. Some texts may refer to this use of *Be* as State of Being. **See also *Copula, Linking Verb,* and *Stative Verb*.**

BE VERB *(Continued)*

Be As an Auxiliary Verb

Sean *is* running down the hill.
progressive tense

Dinner is served.
passive voice

Be forms a part of the progressive tense and passive voice. **See also** *Progressive Tense* **and** *Passive voice.*

Be is an irregular verb. **See the Be Verb Chart in Appendix.**

Case

Subject case:	*He* is my friend.
	Sam ate all the ice cream.
Object case:	Lara gave *me* a *necklace*.
	Yvonne gave a *yo-yo* to *him*.
Possessive case:	*Her* mother makes great pies.
	This is *Juan's* house.

Case shows the position of a noun or pronoun in a sentence. **See also *noun, pronoun, object, possessive, subject,* and *sentence.***

Clause

My dog ate my homework.
A sentence with one clause

Since the team had won,
we all went out for pizza.
A sentence with two clauses

My mother, who still teaches at age 80, believes in hard work because that always makes sense to her.
A sentence with three clauses

A clause has a subject and a predicate. A clause can be a sentence or part of a sentence. A sentence can have more than one clause. **See also *main clause, sentence, subject,* and *predicate.***

> **First Sentence:**
> The subject is *my dog,* and the predicate is *ate my homework.*
>
> **Second Sentence:**
> The subject of the first clause is *the team,* and the predicate of the first clause is *had won.*
> The subject of the second clause is *we* and the predicate is *all went out for pizza.*

COLLECTIVE NOUN/NOUN OF MULTITUDE

The *audience yells* enthusiastically.
collective noun with singular verb

The *audience sit* in awe during our performance.
collective noun with a plural verb

The *staff gives* an excellent birthday party.
collective noun with singular verb

The *staff bake* all the food for the party.
collective noun with a plural verb

A collective noun names a group of persons, places, or things gathered together as a unit. Some collective nouns are *family, government, swarm, committee,* and *crowd.* The collective noun usually takes a singular verb unless the individuals of the group are acting separately. **See also *noun.***

COMMA SPLICE

Hector is from Mexico, he speaks Spanish.

Jack Russell is a crazy dog, he drives me nuts.

> **Without a Comma Splice:**
> Hector is from Mexico and he speaks Spanish.
> Jack Russell is a crazy dog. He drives me nuts.

Whenever two independent clauses are separated by a comma, instead of a conjunction or end punctuation, you have a run-on sentence. This is also known as a comma splice. **See also *independent clause,* and *fused sentence.***

COMMON NOUN

Our *teacher* gave each of us a *book*.
common noun   common noun

The *girl* played the *violin*.
common noun   common noun

I'd like to go to the *beach*.
common noun

That *dog* ran right through our *yard*.
common noun   common noun

A common noun is the name of a set of objects, places, or people. The name *car* is common to millions of automobiles. **See also *noun* and *proper noun*.**

COMPARATIVE AND SUPERLATIVE (ADJECTIVES)

My cousin Betty is *prettier* than I am.
comparative

Tara has *less* hair than Jennifer.
comparative

My mom is the *best* cook in the whole world.
superlative

Matilda is the *prettiest* girl in school.
superlative

The comparative and superlative are forms of adjectives. Comparative shows the comparison of two things. You make the comparative by adding -*er* or using *less, more, worse,* or *better.* Superlative shows the most or least of a group of the same thing. You make the superlative by adding -*est* or using *least, worst, most* or *best.* **See also *adjectives.***

COMPLEX SENTENCE

Because the movie started early, *the couple missed dinner.*
subordinate clause   main clause

The couple missed dinner because the movie started early.
main clause   subordinate clause

A complex sentence has a main clause and at least one subordinate clause. Use a comma after an introductory subordinate clause. **See also *main clause, subordinate clause, clause,* and *sentence.***

COMPOUND ADJECTIVE

My grandfather was a *self-educated* man.
compound adjective

The *heart-wrenching* story was not easily forgotten.
compound adjective

A compound adjective is a compound word. It is two or more adjectives joined by a hyphen and used as one word. **See also *compound word.***

COMPOUND NOUN

My mother always puts *corn syrup* on her pancakes.
compound noun

The *golden retriever* is a beautiful dog.
compound noun

A compound noun is two words used to convey a single idea. Often the two words are both nouns, but together they represent a new idea like *corn syrup*. Sometimes the compound noun has an adjective and a noun used to name something specific like *golden retriever*. Compound nouns usually have a separate entry in the dictionary.

COMPLETE SUBJECT

The boy is running.
noun as the subject

I am going shopping.
pronoun as the subject

The rolling green hills of Kentucky are a beautiful sight.
noun phrase as the subject

The subject generally comes before the predicate and usually is the topic of the sentence. A complete subject is a noun, a pronoun, noun phrase, or a noun clause. **See also *noun, pronoun, noun phrase, noun clause,* and *predicate.***

COMPOUND-COMPLEX SENTENCE

Nate ran after the bus, and Katie waited at the bus stop until the next bus came.

As there are five of us, three should take the trail to the left and two of us can take the trail to the right.

A compound-complex sentence has at least two main clauses connected with a coordinating conjunction and at least one subordinate clause. **See also *clause, coordinating conjunction, main clause,* and *subordinate clause.***

Nate ran after the bus,
main clause

and
coordinating conjunction

Katie waited at the bus stop
main clause

until the next bus came.

As there are five of us,
subordinate clause

three should take the trail to the left
main clause

and
coordinating conjunction

two of us can take the trail to the right.
main clause

COMPOUND PHRASE

Our plan was *simple but workable.*

The children saw a *small, brown, and very furry bunny.*

The *frisky, young horse* trotted toward us.

A compound phrase is words or phrases joined by a conjunction, a comma, or both. **See also *conjunction* and *phrase.***

> These are three examples of how you can use compound phrases in a sentence. Each one has different punctuation.

COMPOUND SENTENCE

The basketball team played Las Cruces last week, and *they play El Paso next week.*

Julia asked for cake, but *Claudia wanted pie.*

A compound sentence has at least two main clauses joined by a comma and coordinating conjunction. **See also *conjunction, coordination,* and *main clause.***

> The basketball team played Las Cruces last week,
>
> **main clause**
>
> and
>
> **coordinating conjunction**
>
> they play El Paso next week.
>
> **main clause**

COMPOUND WORD

My mother always puts *corn syrup* on her pancakes.
            compound word

My grandfather was a *self-educated* man.
            compound word

A compound word is two or more words acting like a single word. Some compound words are *self-made, hand-made, corn flakes,* and *fox trot.*

CONCORD

Concord is another word for agreement. English has two kinds of agreement.

The Cocker Spaniel **jumps** for joy.

singular subject   singular verb

> The subject and verb must agree in number.

The children **play** at the park.

plural subject   plural verb

English has the remnants of an older verb system. In this system, the verb took a different ending for each person. See *Person.* Today, the only change is for third person singular. This includes the pronouns *he, she,* and *it.* These verbs take an "s" ending. **See also *subject, verb, singular,* and *plural.***

Robert is coming to the party. *He* is bringing a pizza.

antecedent   pronoun

Kerensa called to say *she* will be late.

antecedent   pronoun

Sam and Sara said *they* can't come.

antecedent   pronoun

The pronoun and its antecedent must agree in number—singular or plural—and gender—masculine, feminine, or neutral. **See also *antecedent, gender, plural, pronoun,* and *singular.***

CONCRETE NOUN

The boy has a green *vest.*

concrete noun

A concrete noun names physical things. Some concrete nouns are *table, bed, book, boy, girl,* and *car.* **See also *noun.***

CONJOINING

Sam *and* Bill went skiing.
conjunction

Conjoining means connecting. Conjunctions are *conjoining* words. They connect words, phrases, or clauses. **See also *conjunction/ coordinating conjunction.***

CONJUGATION

I *jog* everyday.   He *jogs* after dinner.
third person singular present tense

He *was* a champion prizefighter.

They *were* his biggest fans.

> *Be* changes showing number: *was* for singular and *were* for plural.

I *jog* everyday.

I *jogged* yesterday.

> These sentences show changes in tense.

I *will jog* tomorrow.

Conjugation is the way a verb changes to show tense, number, and person. English has a very reduced form of conjugation. Generally, conjugation in English shows only changes in tense. The exceptions are *Be* and third person singular present tense. **See also *verb, person, number,* and *tense.***

Conjunction/Coordinating Conjunction

Our dance costumes are easy to make *but* beautiful.
conjunction

The dog was hungry, *so* he ate my sandwich.
conjunction

A conjunction joins a word, words, phrases, or clauses. The words *and, but, or, yet,* or *nor* are conjunctions. The only time you use the conjunctions *for* or *so* is to join clauses. Sometimes a conjunction is also called a coordinating conjunction. **See also *clause, coordination,* and *phrase.***

Conjunctive Adverb

The mayor wants to keep the park open; *however,* the city council wants it developed into another mall. *Furthermore,* the council wants to build new streets to support the extra traffic.

A conjunctive adverb is another kind of connecting word. It connects two sentences or main clauses with each other. It shows the relationship between the two clauses. Generally it comes at the beginning of a sentence, but it may come anywhere in the sentence. You find conjunctive adverbs in formal writing and speaking. **See also *Subordinator.***

CONTINUOUS

She *is running* down the hill.

The clown *was tripping* over his own feet.

The elders *will be hiking* throughthe woods tomorrow.

Continuous is another name for progressive. Progressive forms or tenses show continuous action. There are present, past, and future progressive tenses. They are formed by adding some form of the *be* verb to a present participle. **See also *present progressive tense, past progressive tense, future progressive tense, verb, tense,* and *participle.***

COORDINATION

dog and *cat*
noun   noun

magenta or *green*
adjective   adjective

walk or *run*
verb   verb

by the bush or *near the grass*
prepositional phrase   prepositional phrase

She is running, but *he is walking.*
clause   clause

Coordination means that the joined parts are grammatically equal: nouns to nouns, verbs to verbs, prepositional phrases to prepositional phrases, adjectives to adjectives, and clauses to clauses. **See also *noun, verb, prepositional phrase, adjective,* and *clause.***

COPULA

She *is* my mother.

copula

The tablecloth *was* red.

copula

She *smells* sweet.

copula

You *grow* taller every time I see you.

copula

The old willow tree *stands* near a stream.

copula

A copula or linking verb connects a subject to a word or words describing (adjectives), identifying (nouns), or telling the location of (adverbial prepositional phrases) the subject. **See also *Predicate Adjective, Predicate Noun,* and *Phrases.***

COUNTABLE NOUN/COUNT NOUN

The *chicken* crossed the *road.*

countable noun   countable noun

There are three *chickens* in the *coop.*

countable noun   countable noun

A countable noun has both singular and plural forms. You can count them. **See also *noun.***

CORRELATIVES/CORRELATIVE CONJUNCTION

Both Thomas *and* Maria want to go.

Not only do we need to make money, *but also* we need to have some fun.

Either we will go to the movies, *or* we will rent a movie.

Correlatives are words you use in pairs to join words, phrases, or clauses.

See also *conjunctions*.

> Some correlatives are
>
> both...and
> not only...but also
> either...or
> neither...nor
> whether...or

DANGLING MODIFIER

Skipping swiftly toward the door, the table tipped over.
dangling modifier

A dangling modifier is a word or phrase without anything to modify. Modifiers usually come just before or just after the word they are modifying. Dangling modifiers are not typically used in formal writing.
See also *modifier.*

> There is nothing for the phrase *skipping swiftly toward the door* to modify.
>
> You could say
>
> *Skipping swiftly toward the door,* the kids tipped over the table.
>
> Now the phrase modifies *the kids.*

DECLARATIVE SENTENCE

It will rain tomorrow.

Julie likes bagels and cream cheese.

A declarative sentence makes a statement and ends in a period.

DEFINING ADJECTIVE CLAUSE/ RESTRICTIVE RELATIVE CLAUSE

We have a cat *that is a good mouser.*
defining adjective clause

A defining adjective clause is essential for the meaning of the sentence. When you leave it out, the sentence has a different meaning.
See also *clause, main clause,* **and** *adjective clause.* **See also the Defining and Non-Defining Adjective Clauses chart in the Appendix.**

> Without the clause *that is a good mouser,* the sentence has a different meaning.
>
> We have a cat.
>
> By adding the clause, you define *cat.* The clause is not separated from *cat* by a

DEFINITE ARTICLE

The black cat ran in front of my car.
definite article

Please hand me *the* book with the brown cover.
definite article

The rich have it easy.
definite article

We live in *the* United States.
definite article

> You use *the* with an adjective to make the adjective a noun.
>
> You use *the* as part of a title or proper noun.

The is a definite article. When you refer to a specific noun, you use the definite article. *A* and *an* are indefinite articles. When you refer to any noun you use an indefinite article. *The* is a weakened form of *that*. You use *the* with singular nouns to show the kind of object. **See also *indefinite article, article, adjective, noun* and *proper noun.***

DEFINITE PRONOUN

Mr. Tran whistled as *he* worked.
antecedent   definite pronoun

Since *she* likes chocolate, *Auntie Em* baked brownies.
definite pronoun   antecedent

A definite pronoun has an antecedent either before or shortly after it. **See also *antecedent* and *pronoun.***

DEMONSTRATIVE ADJECTIVE

Mother bought *these* new shoes yesterday.
demonstrative adjective

That dessert is my favorite.
demonstrative adjective

A demonstrative adjective is a demonstrative pronoun used as an adjective. **See also** *adjective, pronoun, adjective pronoun,* **and** *demonstrative pronoun.*

DEMONSTRATIVE PRONOUN

Those are mine.
demonstrative pronoun

That book belongs to Bill.
demonstrative pronoun

These cookies are great.
demonstrative pronoun

This isn't my dad's shirt.
demonstrative pronoun

> *That* and *those* say things are far from the speaker. Use *that* for singular and *those* for plural.
>
> *This* and *these* say things are near to the speaker. Use *this* for singular and *these* for plural.

A demonstrative pronoun tells whether something is near to or far from the speaker. **See also** *demonstrative adjective* **and** *pronoun.*

DEPENDENT CLAUSE

My mother knew *that I would be home by curfew.*

> The dependent clause is a noun clause.

My daughter, *who has several children of her own,* still works full time.

> The dependent clause is an adjective clause.

My mother lives in Arkansas *where she was born.*

> The dependent clause is an adverbial clause.

A dependent clause gives information about the independent clause. It has a subject and a predicate, but it does not have much meaning without the independent clause. It's meaning is dependent on the independent clause. It may be a noun clause, an adjective clause, or an adverbial clause. A dependent clause is also called a *subordinate clause.* **See also *independent clause, main clause, subject, predicate, noun clause, adjective clause,* and *adverbial clause.***

DIRECT OBJECT

Hank hit *the ball.*
     direct object

Mom baked *the cake.*
     direct object

My friend drew *the picture with the leopards on it.*
          direct object

Ricky wrote *that he was coming home.*
          direct object

A direct object tells who or what directly receives the action of the verb. A direct object can be a noun, a pronoun, a noun phrase, or a noun clause. **See also *noun, pronoun, noun phrase, object,* and *transitive verb.***

DOUBLE NEGATIVE

He *never* saw *nothing*.

People use double negatives to show emphasis or for characterization. A double negative does not become a positive.

A sentence with a double negative uses two negative words. Double negatives are not typically used in formal writing. (You could say, *he saw nothing,* or *he didn't see anything.*)

EMBEDDING

Aunt Sue, *who had just returned from Japan,* showed slides from her trip.

Sentence 1: Aunt Sue showed slides from her trip.

Sentence 2: Who (Aunt Sue) had just returned from Japan.

Embedding is the action of putting one sentence or clause within another sentence. Sentence 2 is embedded in Sentence 1. You can use this technique to make complex sentences. **See also *complex sentence* and *clause.***

EXCLAMATORY SENTENCE

How clever **he** *can* be!
    subject auxiliary verb

What a great movie!
    phrase

Exclamatory sentences begin with a phrase using *what* or *how,* but they do not reverse the order of the subject and the auxiliary verb. Some exclamatory sentences may just be a phrase using *what* or *how.* **See also *subject, auxiliary verb, phrase,* and *sentence.***

Expletive

There **will be** no rain tomorrow for our game.
expletive linking verb   subject

It **is** likely that we will have fried chicken for lunch.
expletive linking verb   subject

An expletive comes before a
linking verb when the linking verb
is followed by the subject.
See also *linking verb* **and** *subject.*

The words *it* and *there* are
called dummy subjects or
expletives. They are not the
subject of the sentences, they
just appear where you
normally find the subject.

FAULTY PARALLELISM

I want to live with *simplicity*, good *humor*, and *logically*.
noun   noun   adverb

When connecting words, use the same form. Join nouns with nouns, adjectives with adjectives, verbs with verbs, adverbs with adverbs, and phrases with phrases. When you mix these, you get faulty parallelism.
See also *noun, verb, adjective, adverb, phrase,* and *parallel construction.*

> *Simplicity* and *humor* are both nouns whereas *logically* is an adverb. The words all tell how I want to live but they don't all have the same form.

> **You can change it to this.**
>
> I want to live with *simplicity,* good *humor,* and *logic.*
> noun   noun   noun

FAULTY TENSE SHIFT

I *made* a cake, but I *leave* it at home.
past tense   present tense

When she *arrives*, I *served* red chile.
present tense   past tense

> The sentences should read
>
> I made a cake, but I left it at home.
>
> When she arrived, I served red chile.

A faulty tense shift happens when you inappropriately shift from one tense to another within the same sentence. **See also *verb, present tense, past tense,* and *future tense.***

FIRST PERSON

I like chocolate candy bars.   Look at *me*.

That is *my* best tablecloth.   *We* are late!

Personal and possessive pronouns have person. First person shows who is speaking. *See pronoun, personal pronoun,* **and** *person.*

FRAGMENT

A single apple from the tree.

Falling down.

A single apple fell. On my head.

A single apple fell. Because the wind blew it down.

A sentence fragment is often an incomplete sentence because the end punctuation was incorrectly done. Sometimes a period, question mark, or exclamation mark breaks a sentence into fragments.

FUSED SENTENCE

The airplanes whined overhead they were dropping leaflets.

A fused sentence is two sentences put together without any conjunction, subordinator, or punctuation. Fused sentences are not typically used in formal writing. **See also** *sentence.*

FUTURE PERFECT TENSE

We *will have finished* our practice by 3 p.m.
    past participle

We *will have eaten* all our snacks by the time we arrive.
    past participle

You make future perfect tense by using *will* + *have* + the past participle. **See also *participle* and *tense*.**

You use future perfect tense to say an action will be completed by the time something else happens.

You use future perfect tense to say an action will be completed by a specified time in the future.

FUTURE TENSE

She *will make* lasagna for dinner.

We *will go* to dinner around 6 p.m.

You use future tense to show an action will happen in the future. You make future tense by using *will* + the base form of the verb. **See also *present tense*, *past tense*, and *verb*.**

GENDER

The coach gave *him his* award.

It is my book.

Where did *she* go?

Personal pronouns have three genders. They can be masculine (he, him), feminine (she, her), and neuter (it). **See also *agreement* and *pronoun*.**

GENITIVE CASE

Give *your* grandmother a hug.

The *earth's* surface is mostly water.

Curtis' dog is a Scottish Terrier.

Genitive case is possessive case. It shows possession, origin, or a similar relationship. English shows genitive or possessive case by adding an "s" or "z" sound or by using possessive pronouns. **See also *possession, pronoun, noun,* and *prepositional phrase*.**

GERUND

Swimming is an aerobic activity.
gerund or verbal noun

I like *swimming* in the afternoons.
gerund or verbal noun

A gerund is a verbal noun. It is the present participle used as a noun. It has some properties of both a noun and a verb. **See also *verb, participle,* and *noun*.**

GERUND PHRASE

Biking through the hills is a great way to spend a day.
gerund phrase

Being active helps people live longer.
gerund phrase

A gerund phrase is a gerund plus any objects, modifiers, or both. Like a verb, you can use it with an adverbial prepositional phrase, an object, a predicate adjective, or a predicate noun. **See *also* *verb, objects, predicate adjectives, and predicate nouns.***

GRAMMAR

Grammar is the study of how words and phrases come together to make sentences. It includes all the rules for how to make sentences.

Helping (Auxiliary) verb

A helping verb is an auxiliary verb.

Creating Tense

Grandmother *will* leave tomorrow.
helping verb

Creating Mood

Our math teacher *may* give us a test today.
helping verb

Creating Voice

The football game *was* played on Saturday.
helping verb

You add a helping verb to the base form of a verb or participle to make more tenses and to show mood or voice. Auxiliary means giving assistance or help. Some helping (auxiliary) verbs are *have, may, can, must,* and *will.* **See the Modal Auxiliary Verb chart in the Appendix for a more complete understanding. See also** *verb, base form, tense, mood, participle,* **and** *voice.*

IMPERATIVE MOOD

Go to bed!

Stand up!

Stay, Finnegan!

Mood is a form of a verb. Mood tells the writer's or speaker's attitude about the statement. There are three moods. A verb in the imperative mood states actuality or strong probability. **See also *mood, verb,* and *modal auxiliary verb.***

IMPERATIVE SENTENCE

Pick up your clothes.　　Let us begin class.
　　command　　　　　　　　　request

An imperative sentence usually gives a command or makes a request. The subject of a command may be the implied subject *you.* **See also *sentence* and *subject.***

INDEFINITE ARTICLE

I need *a* raincoat.
　indefinite article

Please hand me *an* egg from the refrigerator.
　　　　　definite article

A and *an* are indefinite articles. They are two forms of the same word. *An* is the earlier form. Today, you use *an* before vowel sounds only. It is the unstressed form of *one.* It shows one of a general class. When you mean *any,* you use *a* or *an.* **See also *definite article* and *article.***

INDEPENDENT CLAUSE

The boy who kicked the winning goal *was only fifteen.*

The independent clause or main clause is part of a complex sentence. The independent clause is understandable by itself. See also *clause* and *complex sentence.*

> You can understand the independent clause—*the boy was only fifteen*— without the other clause. You cannot understand the clause—*who kicked the winning goal*—without the independent clause.

INDICATIVE MOOD

Dinner *will be* at 6 PM. We *are having* roast chicken.

Do you *like* roast chicken?

Mood is a form of a verb telling the writer's or speaker's attitude about the statement. English has three moods. The indicative mood states actuality or strong probability. See also *mood, verb,* and *modal auxiliary verb.*

INDIRECT OBJECT

I gave *Juan* a football.
  indirect object

Giselle handed *the puppy* a bone.
  indirect object

Sara wrote *me* a letter.
  indirect object

> Some verbs that take an indirect object are *give, grant, ask, allow, pay, loan, hand, send, allot, offer, write, tell, teach, furnish,* and *get.*

An indirect object receives the action of the verb indirectly. You can have an indirect object only if you have a direct object. See also *direct object* and *verb.*

INFINITIVE

To write is my life.
infinitive

I live *to write.*
infinitive

You may *come* in.
infinitive

To have fallen down during the race was awful.
present perfect infinitive

She wanted *to be recognized* for her grades.
present tense/passive voice

> An infinitive may have tenses and voice.

The infinitive is the base form of the verb. In English, you often see it with *to.* You can use the infinitive several ways in English, including with auxiliary verbs or as a noun. **See also *verb, participle,* and *noun.***

INFINITIVE PHRASE

I love *to bike through the hills.*
infinitive phrase

The infinitive is the base form of the verb. In English, you often see it with *to.* You can use the infinitive several ways in English, including with auxiliary verbs or as a noun. Like a verb, the infinitive may take an adverbial prepositional phrase, object, predicate adjective, or predicate noun. **See also *objects, prepositional phrase, predicate adjective,* and *predicate noun.***

INTENSIFIER

He made us laugh *loudly*.
intensifier

Uncle Pat told *very* interesting stories.
intensifier

> Use an exclamation mark for strong feeling and a comma for weaker feeling.

An intensifier is a word or group of words intensifying another word or group of words in a sentence. To intensify is to increase or make greater in some way. Intensifiers are usually adverbs or adjectives.

INTERJECTIONS

Ugh, I hate chocolate milk.   *Gosh!* This is delicious.
interjection   interjection

An interjection is a word added to a sentence to show emotion or attitude. It is independent of the sentence. Interjections may show delight, surprise, shock, pain, warning, approval, disapproval, or disgust.

INTERROGATIVE PRONOUN

To *whom* do you wish to speak?
interrogative pronoun

Whose shoe is this?
interrogative pronoun

Interrogative pronouns usually begin with *wh-*. You use them to make questions. The interrogative pronouns are *what, who, which, whose,* and *whom*. **See also *pronoun*.**

INTERROGATIVE SENTENCE

Do you like cucumbers?

Is this your shirt?

What kind of pizza do you want?

Where is my new hat?

An interrogative sentence asks a question and ends with a question mark. **See also** *sentence.*

INTRANSITIVE VERB

Jack and Jill *ran* up the hill.
intransitive verb

After school, we can *walk* home.
intransitive verb

> *Up the hill* and *home* are both adverbial phrases telling where.

An intransitive verb does not have a direct object. It does not transfer or carry the action from the subject to an object. **See also** *verb, subject, direct object,* **and** *adverbial phrase.*

INTRODUCTORY CLAUSE

Before you go to bed, take your shoes off.

Whenever you hear this bell, you need to sit down.

An introductory clause comes before the main clause of the sentence. It is a dependent or subordinate clause. **See also** *dependent clause* **and** *subordinate clause.*

INTRODUCTORY PHRASE

Like his brother, he makes great cherry pies.

At noon tomorrow, we will meet at the cafe.

An introductory phrase is a group of words coming before the subject but not modifying the subject. **See also** *phrase.*

INTRODUCTORY WORD

Then, Joe stood up and walked away.

Finally, the bus pulled out two hours late.

An introductory word comes before the subject. It is usually a sentence modifier. **See also** *adverb.*

IRREGULAR VERB

We *hid* the diamond necklace in the freezer.
<small>irregular verb</small>

The bus *left* the terminal late.
<small>irregular verb</small>

Irregular verbs usually come from Old English. They form their past tense and past participle using older forms. Regular verbs form their past tense and past participle by adding *-ed.* **See also** *participle, past tense, verb,* **and the Irregular Verbs chart in the Appendix.**

LIMITER

We had *barely* five dollars.
limiter

This is an event for children *only*.
limiter

A limiter is an adverb. You use it to limit the meaning of the word immediately before it. *Almost, hardly, just, only, barely,* and *nearly* are limiters. **See also *adverb* and *modifier.***

LINKING VERB

She *is* my mother.
linking verb

The tablecloth *was* red.
linking verb

She *smells* sweet.
linking verb

You *grow* taller every time I see you.
linking verb

The primary linking verb is *be* in its various forms: *be, am, is, are, was, were.* You can use other verbs as linking verbs. Some of these are *feel, look, prove, remain, resemble, sound, stay, become, grow, turn, smell,* and *taste.*

A linking verb or copula connects a subject to a word or words describing (adjectives), identifying (nouns), or telling the location of (adverbial prepositional phrases) the subject. **See also *Predicate Adjective, Predicate Noun,* and *Phrases.***

MAIN CLAUSE

The boy who kicked the
winning goal *was only fifteen.*

The main clause or independent
clause is part of a complex sentence.
The main clause is understandable
by itself. **See also *Clause* and
*Complex Sentence.***

> You can understand
> the main clause—*the
> boy was only fifteen*—
> without the other
> clause. You cannot
> understand the
> clause—*who kicked the
> winning goal*—without
> the main clause.

MASS NOUN

A good *education* is worth millions.
      mass noun

A noun without singular and plural forms. You cannot count it.
Some mass nouns are *harm, homework,* and *simplicity.*
See also *noun.*

MISPLACED MODIFIER

Running swiftly down the hill, the race was won by Al.
    misplaced modifier

A misplaced modifier does not
come just before or after the word
it modifies. **See also *modifier.***

> The modifier *running swiftly
> down the hill* goes right after
> *Wesley.* The race was won by
> Wesley, *running swiftly down
> the hill.*

MODAL/MODAL AUXILIARY

We *should* be home soon.

modal auxiliary

Julie *can* speak six languages.

modal auxiliary

A modal auxiliary verb indicates the subjunctive mood of the verb. Some of these are *should, can, would, could, may, might, must,* and *ought*. **See also *auxiliary verb, subjunctive mood, verb,* and the Modal Auxiliary Verb chart in the Appendix.**

MODE/MOOD

Dinner *will be* at 6 PM.

We *are having* roast chicken.

Do you *like* roast chicken?

> **Indicative Mode
> (Stating Facts)**
>
> A verb in indicative mood states actuality or strong probability.

Go to bed!

Stand up!

Stay, Finnegan!

> **Imperative Mode
> (Giving Commands or Making Requests)**
>
> A verb in imperative mood commands or makes requests directly.

If I *were* a sparrow, I *would* fly away.

You *should eat* something now.

> **Subjunctive Mode
> (Expressing Possibility or Suggestion)**
>
> A verb in subjunctive mood suggests, wishes, recommends, requires, or guesses. A verb in subjunctive mood may change its form, or it may take a modal auxiliary verb.

English has three modes. Mode is another word for mood. The mode or mood of the verb tells the writer's or speaker's attitude about the statement. **See also *verb* and *modal auxiliary verb*.**

Modifier

He made us laugh *loudly*.   We thought he was *great*.
               modifier   modifier

Beaming at us, he would begin another tale.
   modifier

Uncle Pat told *very interesting* stories.
               modifier

A modifier is a word or group of words describing or limiting another word or group of words in a sentence.

NOMINAL

Nominal is another name for a noun. **See also *noun.***

NOMINAL CLAUSE/NOUN CLAUSE

The Senator thought
that taxes should be lower.
noun clause

> Subject: taxes
> Predicate: should be lower

Whoever wants pizza raise your hands.
noun clause

This song is dedicated to *whoever loves to dance.*
noun clause

A noun clause has a subject and a predicate. It takes the noun place in a sentence. It can be a subject, a direct object, a predicate noun, or an object of a preposition. **See also *direct object, predicate noun, object of a preposition, noun, subject,* and *predicate.***

> Noun clauses can start with *that, what, whatever, who, which, whoever, whomever,* and sometimes *how, when,* and *where.*

NON-DEFINING ADJECTIVE CLAUSE/ NON-RESTRICTIVE RELATIVE CLAUSE

We have a cat, *which we love very much.*
non-defining adjective clause

Alfred, *who eats lots of sugar,* has many cavities.
non-defining adjective clause

A non-defining adjective clause is not essential for the meaning of the sentence; it simply adds additional information. When you leave it out, the sentence still has the basic meaning. See also clause, main clause, and adjective clause. **See the *Defining* and *Non-Defining Adjective Clauses* chart in the Appendix.**

NOUN

Mother bought a new *table*.   *Love* is difficult to define.
noun   noun   noun

Our *class* visited the *Natural History Museum*.
    noun   noun

A noun names things, persons, ideas, and places.

NOUN CLAUSE/NOMINAL CLAUSE

The Senator thought *that taxes should be lower*.
              noun clause

Whoever wants pizza raise your hands.
noun clause

This song is dedicated to *whoever loves to dance*.
                           noun clause

A noun clause has a subject and a predicate. It takes the noun place in a sentence. It can be a subject, a direct object, a predicate noun, or an object of a preposition. **See also *direct object, nominal clause, predicate noun, object of a preposition, noun, subject,* and *predicate*.**

NOUN EQUIVALENT

Running is a form of aerobic exercise.
noun equivalent

She hopes *that we will go camping*.
           noun equivalent

Running verbal noun
that we will go camping noun clause

A noun equivalent is a verbal noun or a noun clause. **See also *noun, verbal noun,* and *noun clause*.**

Noun Phrase

A slimy, green wiggle worm is crawling up *the old oak tree.*
noun phrase   noun phrase

A tall, blue giant gave **the little boy** *a gray and white pony.*
noun phrase   noun phrase   noun phrase

The barking dog is *a very unhappy German Shepherd.*
noun phrase   noun phrase

A noun phrase is a group of words taking the place of a noun in a sentence. A noun phrase can be a subject, indirect object, direct object, a predicate noun, or an object of a preposition. A noun phrase may be a single noun or a pronoun. A noun phrase can include its modifiers. **See also *noun, pronoun, subject, indirect object, direct object, predicate noun, object of a preposition,* and *phrase.***

Number

The four *boys* from the track team want to order six pepperoni and black olive *pizzas.* One *boy* wants a green chile *pizza. They* are very hungry.

Number tells whether a word is singular or plural. You mostly see this with nouns or pronouns. **See also *singular* and *plural.***

Object/Object of the Preposition

James kicked *the ball.*   The squirrel ran up *the tree.*

transitive verb   object

preposition   object

Nouns and pronouns can be the object of transitive verbs and prepositions. **See also *transitive verb, direct object,* and *preposition.***

Object Case/Objective Case

The waiter gave *them* the wrong order.

This check is for *him.*

A noun or pronoun used as a direct object, indirect object, or object of a preposition is in object case. Personal pronouns change form when they are indirect objects, direct objects, or objects of prepositions. **See also *personal pronouns.***

> **Compare**
> *They* **got the wrong order from the waiter.** **This is *his* check.**

Parallel Construction

We must *take a risk* or *lose our business*.

> phrase with phrase

For dinner we had *peas, carrots, celery, potatoes,* and *ham*.

> noun with noun

The room was *spacious* and *charming*.

> adjective with adjective

The CEO spoke *softly* but *clearly* about the future of the company.

> adverb with adverb

Yesterday the boys *jogged, swam,* and *biked*.

> verb with verb

We know *that they like to hike, that they like to boat,* and *that they expect to do both*.

> clause with clause

You use parallel construction in your sentences when you arrange nouns with nouns, adjectives with adjectives, adverbs with adverbs, verbs with verbs, phrase with phrase, and clause with clause. **See also** *faulty parallelism, phrase, noun, adjective, adverb, verb,* and *clause*.

PARTICIPLE

Running swiftly, the Rio Grande twists and turns through the narrow canyon. | participle acting as an adjective

The swiftly running Rio Grande twists and turns through the narrow canyon. | participle acting as an adjective

Running is an aerobic activity. | participle acting as a noun

The deer *are running* gracefully through the trees. | present participle in present perfect tense

You make present participles by adding *–ing* to the base form of the verb.

Over the mountains lies a *hidden* canyon. | participle acting as an adjective

The jewels *were hidden* in the old refrigerator. | past participle in passive voice

We *have hidden* the jewels in the old refrigerator. | past participle in present perfect tense

You make past participles for regular verbs by adding *–ed* to the base form. Irregular verbs make a variety of changes to form their past participles.

A participle is a verb form used as a noun, an adjective, or to form the progressive and perfect tenses and passive voice. **See also *verbal, participle, present participle, participle phrase, progressive tense, perfect tense, passive voice,* and *adjective.* See the Irregular Verb chart in the Appendix.**

PARTICIPLE PHRASE

Running swiftly, the Rio Grande twists and turns through the narrow canyon.

> participle: ***Running***
> its modifier: ***swiftly***

Pulling the rotten tooth, the dentist grinned with satisfaction.

> participle: ***Pulling***
> its object: ***the rotten***

A participle phrase contains a participle, its object, its modifiers, or both. Participles like verbs can take an object. **See *participle, phrase, verbal, modifier,* and *object.***

PARTS OF SPEECH

Mr. Jones eats *grapes* for *breakfast* everyday.

There is a *nest* in the attic.

We found two *nests* in one tree.

Mr. Jones eats *grapes* for *breakfast.*

Mr. Jones is *my favorite teacher.*

> **Meaning**
> A noun names a person, place, or thing.
>
> **Form**
> A noun has both a singular and plural form.
>
> **Function**
> A noun can be a subject, an object, or a predicate noun.

Parts of speech is a traditional grammar term. It describes the types of words used to make a sentence.

You can identify parts of speech in three different ways: by its meaning, by its form, or by its function. The parts of speech are nouns, pronouns, adjectives, verbs, adverbs, conjunctions, prepositions, and sometimes interjections.

PASSIVE VOICE

The ball *was hit by* Joe.

The cake *was eaten by* Nick.

> In passive voice, the subject is acted upon. In passive voice, the action moves back to the subject.

Voice indicates whether the subject acts or is acted upon. Only transitive verbs can make a change in voice. **See also *subject, transitive verb,* and *direct object.***

PAST PARTICIPLE

The jewels *were hidden* in the old refrigerator.

We *have hidden* the jewels in the old refrigerator.

They *had walked* for miles.

The past participle is a verb form. You make it by adding -ed to the base form of the verb except for some older verbs called irregular verbs. You use a past participle to form the perfect tenses and passive voice or as an adjective. **See also *participle, passive voice,* and *perfect tenses.***

PAST PERFECT TENSE

By midnight we *had finished* the party.

They *had eaten* dinner before we arrived.

> You use past perfect tense to say an action or state was completed by a specified time in the past. You use past perfect tense to show one action was completed by the time another past action or state happened.

Past perfect tense shows the relationship between two actions in the past. You make past perfect tense by using *had* + the past participle. **See also *participle, verb,* and *tense.***

PAST TENSE

The rainbow *appeared* after the storm.

> You use past tense to report an action or state definitely over in the past.

My family *had* fried chicken every Sunday for lunch.

> You use past tense to report actions done repeatedly in the past but no longer being done.

Past tense shows an action or state happened in the past. **See also *tense* and *verb*.**

PERFECT PARTICIPLE

Having called the president, the senator described his plan for better education.

> *called* is the past participle

You make a perfect participle by using *having* or *having been* + the past participle. **See also *participle*.**

PERFECT TENSE

He *has called* three times.

> present perfect tense

They *had waited* for a bus for two hours before they called a cab.

> past perfect tense

We *will have finished* our homework before the game starts.

> future perfect tense

You use a perfect tense to show a relationship in time between two actions or states. **See *tense*, *future perfect tense*, *past perfect tense*, and *present perfect tense*.**

PERSON

I like chocolate candy bars.

Look at *me*.

That is *my* best table cloth.

We are late!

> Person shows who is speaking (first person),

You should take Spanish next year.

Is this *your* book?

> who is being spoken to (second person),

He plays on the soccer team.

She went to *their* house for dinner.

They went to the movies on Friday.

> and who is being spoken about (third person).

Personal and possessive pronouns have person. Person shows who is speaking, who is being spoken to, or who is being spoken about. **See pronoun and *personal pronoun*.**

PERSONAL PRONOUNS

I like her new dress.

The boys mowed *our* lawn.

Give this cake to *them*.

> The personal pronouns are *I, me, we, us, you, he, him, she, her, it, they,* and *them*. The possessive forms of the personal pronouns are *my, mine, our, ours, his, her, hers, its, your, yours, their,* and *theirs*.

Personal pronouns refer to persons or things. They have gender, number, and person. **See also *gender, number, person, pronoun,* and *possessive*.**

PHRASE

A phrase is a group of words functioning as a unit. There can be noun phrases, participle phrases, verb phrases, prepositional phrases, adjective phrases, and adverbial phrases.

The bride caught *her long white train* on *a nail.*

> A noun phrase has a noun plus all its modifiers. It may also be a single noun or a pronoun. (see *noun phrase*)

Catching her long white train on a nail, the bride tripped.

> A participle phrase has a participle, its object, its modifiers, or both. (see *participle phrase*)

The bride *caught her long white train on a nail.*

> A verb phrase has a verb, its objects, its modifiers, or both. Another name for verb phrase is a predicate.

The bride caught her long white train *on a nail.*

> A prepositional phrase has a preposition and its object. You can use a prepositional phrase as an adjective or adverb. (see *prepositional phrase*)

The boy scout troop took a *very slow* train through Tibet.

> An adjective phrase has an adjective or an adjective plus its modifiers.

The train climbed *very slowly* up the mountain.

> An adverb phrase is a word or group of words telling *where, when, how,* and *why.*

PLURAL

The *boys* ordered six pepperoni *pizzas*.
plural noun   plural noun

They also ordered three *pitchers* of root beer.
plural pronoun   plural noun

Plural means there are two or more of something. Some nouns and pronouns have plural forms. Some remain the same for singular or plural. **See *nouns* and *pronouns.***

POSSESSION/POSSESSIVE

Give *your* grandmother a hug.

> The possessive pronouns are *my, mine, our, ours, his, her, hers, its, your, yours, their,* and *theirs.*

Mary's horse won the race.

> With singular nouns, you add an *'s* to show possession.

Curtis' dog is a Collie.

> With nouns ending in *s,* you add an *'* to show possession.

He is a man *of very few words.*

> Use a prepositional phrase beginning with *of* to show possession.

There are several ways to show possession or ownership. **See also *pronoun, noun,* and *prepositional phrase.***

PREDICATE

The boy *ran.*

predicate

The boy *ran swiftly down the hill.*

predicate

The tall boy with blond hair *ran swiftly down the hill.*

predicate

A predicate is a sentence part. It usually begins with a verb and comes right after the subject. A predicate has a verb, its modifiers, its objects, or both. **See also *sentence* and *direct object.***

PREDICATE ADJECTIVE

The lawn is *green.*

predicate adjective

Mr. Garcia seems *sad* today.

predicate adjective

prepositional phrase used as an adverb

prepositional phrase used as an adjective

A predicate adjective follows a linking verb and describes the subject. It is an adjective found within the predicate.

PREDICATE NOMINATIVE /PREDICATE NOUN

My math teacher is also *my soccer coach.*

predicate nominative

A girl will become *a woman.*

predicate noun

A predicate nominative is a predicate noun. It completes the predicate of a linking verb and identifies the subject. It is a noun, noun phrase, or verbal noun. **See also *noun, phrase,* or *verbal.***

PREPOSITION

The cat belongs *to* my friend.
<small>preposition</small>

He is *near* the door.
<small>preposition</small>

They went *over* the fence.
<small>preposition</small>

The students walked *around* the building.
<small>preposition</small>

A preposition shows connections between nouns, pronouns, and verbals to other words in the sentence. **See also *noun, pronoun, verbal,* and the Preposition chart in the Appendix.**

PREPOSITIONAL PHRASE

We ran *down the hill.*
<small>prepositional phrase</small>

Use the room *on the left.*
<small>prepositional phrase</small>

Please do not walk *under the ladder.*
<small>prepositional phrase</small>

A prepositional phrase has a preposition and its object. You can use a prepositional phrase as an adjective or adverb. **See also *adverb, adjective, object,* and *preposition.***

PRESENT PARTICIPLE

Running swiftly, the Rio Grande twists and turns through the narrow canyon.

The swiftly running Rio Grande twists and turns through the narrow canyon.

Running is an aerobic activity.

The deer *are running* gracefully through the trees.

A present participle is a verb form used as a noun or an adjective. It is used to form the progressive and perfect tenses. **See also** *verbal, participle, participle phrase, progressive tense, perfect tense,* **and** *adjective.* **See the Irregular Verb chart in the Appendix.**

PRESENT PERFECT TENSE

Amelia *has been* my best friend since second grade.

> You use present perfect tense to report an action begun in the past and extending into the present.

I *have* just *finished* writing this sentence.

> You use present perfect tense to report a past action relating to something in the present.

The Millers *have finished* their dinner.

> You use present perfect tense to report an action completed at some unspecified time in the past.

You make the present perfect tense by using *have* or *has* + the past participle. **See also** *tense* **and** *participle.*

PRESENT TENSE

I *jump* rope every morning.

> You use present tense to report what happens habitually.

The sun *rises* in the east.

> You use present tense to state a fact or widely held belief.

On Golden Girls, Rose *plays* the dumb roommate.

> You use present tense to describe characters, events, or settings in paintings, pieces of music, literature, a movie, or a television program.

Grandpa John *thinks* his granddaughter is brilliant.

> You use present tense to describe an opinion or idea.

Steinbeck *captures* the variety of life in America in his book Travels with Charley.

> You use present tense to describe what a writer or artist does in creative works.

Aunt Roberta *loves* to dance.

> You use present tense for a condition or situation you expect to last.

School *begins* tomorrow.

> You use present tense for predictable future actions.

Mom says, "When one door *closes,* another *opens.*"

> You use present tense for statements of lasting quality.

Verbs show tense or time. You can use present tense to report or state things several ways. **See also *verb* and *tense.***

PRINCIPLE CLAUSE

The boy who kicked the winning goal *was only fifteen.*

The principal clause is the main clause. It is part of a complex sentence. The principal clause is understandable by itself. Some grammars call this the independent clause. **See also *clause* and *complex sentence.***

PROGRESSIVE TENSES/PROGRESSIVE FORMS

She *is running* down the hill.

> present progressive tense

The clown *was tripping* over his own feet.

> past progressive tense

The elders *will be hiking* through the woods tomorrow.

> future progressive tense

Progressive forms or tenses show continuous action. There are present, past, and future progressive tenses. They are formed by adding some form of the be verb to a present participle. **See also *present progressive tense, past progressive tense, future progressive tense, verb, tense,* and *participle.***

PRONOUN

There are several kinds of pronouns.

She will come with *us*.
His shirt is dirty.

> Personal pronouns refer to persons or things. They have gender, number, and person (see *personal pronoun*).

Those are mine.
This isn't my dad's shirt.

> A demonstrative pronoun tells whether something is near to or far from the speaker (see *demonstrative pronoun*).

To *whom* will you speak?
Whose shoe is this?

> The interrogative pronouns are *what, who, which, whose,* and *whom* (see *interrogative pronoun*). Interrogative pronouns begin with *wh-*. Use them to make questions.

That is *her* kitten.
Is this *yours?*

> A possessive pronoun shows ownership. The possessive pronouns are *my, mine, his, her, hers, its, our, ours, your, yours, their, theirs,* and *whose* (see *possession/possessive*).

The artist praised *himself*.
The baby dressed *herself*.

> A reflexive pronoun is used to direct the action back to the subject (see *reflexive pronoun*).

Her dog, *who* is afraid of water, loves the beach.

The chef made the dish *that* won the contest.

> Relative pronouns introduce adjective clauses. Some relative pronouns are *that, which, who, whose,* and *whom* (see *adjective clause* and *relative pronoun*).

A pronoun takes the place of a noun. **See also *noun*.**

PRONOUN-ANTECEDENT AGREEMENT

Robert is coming to the party. *He* is bringing a pizza.
antecedent   pronoun

Kerensa called to say *she* will be late.
antecedent   pronoun

Sam and Sara said *they* can't come.
antecedent   pronoun

The pronoun and its antecedent must agree in number and gender. **See also *antecedent, gender, plural, pronoun,* and *singular.***

PROPER NOUN

Mr. Nguyen teaches physics at *Central High*.
proper noun   proper noun

Islam is a major religion in *Iran*.
proper noun   proper noun

Ben, Sara, and *Bruce* will all go to *New York*.
proper nouns   proper noun   proper noun

A proper noun is an individual name. The name is distinctive to a person, place, idea, or thing. **See also *noun* and *common noun.***

QUALIFIER

The kitten mewed *quietly*.
qualifier

Juliana is a *beautiful* girl.
qualifier

The *old* house is in need of repair.
qualifier

A qualifier is another name for modifier. **See also *modifier.***

QUANTIFIER

A *few* of us went hiking.
quantifier

There is *plenty* of water.
quantifier

A quantifier is a modifier describing quantity. Some quantifiers are *many, few, little, several, much, a lot of, plenty of, a piece of, a loaf of,* and *three pounds of.* **See also *modifier.***

QUESTION

You can make questions in four ways.

Why are we having spaghetti tonight?

> You can use a question word like *what, when, where,* and *why* (see *interrogative pronoun*).

Can we have spaghetti tonight?

> You can begin the sentence with an auxiliary verb. These are yes-no questions (see *auxiliary verb*).

We are having spaghetti tonight?

> You can change the emphasis in the sentence. The end of the sentence goes up slightly in tone.

We are having spaghetti tonight, *aren't we?*

> You can use a question tag at the end of a sentence. *Aren't we* is a question tag. Other question tags are *isn't it, is it, can he, won't she,* and *do you.*

A question is a kind of sentence. This sentence addresses the listener or reader and asks for an expression of fact, opinion, or belief. You put a question mark at the end of a question. **See also *sentence.***

REFLEXIVE PRONOUN

Today, my little sister dressed *herself*.
reflexive pronoun

A reflexive pronoun is used to direct the action back to the subject. **See also *pronoun*.**

REGULAR VERB

The dog *barked* at the postal delivery person.
regular verb

Andrea *walked* to the post office.
regular verb

I *have played* the violin for my daughter at least once.
regular verb used as a past participle

A regular verb forms its past tense and past participle by adding *-ed* to the base form. Many of these verbs were made from nouns. **See also *verb, noun,* and *verbal*.**

RELATIVE CLAUSE

My mother, *who is eighty years old,* still teaches school.
Non-defining relative clause

He chose the shoe *that had the best arch support*.
defining relative clause

A relative clause is an adjective clause. It modifies a noun. It usually begins with a relative pronoun, a word relating or connecting the relative clause to a noun or noun phrase coming before it. (In the above examples, the relative pronouns are *who* and *that*.) **See also *clause, pronoun,* and *subordinator*.**

RELATIVE PRONOUN

Ellen, *who* is never late, never arrived.
relative pronoun

Ann chose the loan *that* had the best interest rate.
relative pronoun

A relative pronoun begins a relative clause. It shows the relationship between a noun and the clause following it. It is both a pronoun and a connecting word. Relative pronouns also introduce noun clauses. **See the Relative Pronoun Chart in the Appendix.**

RESTRICTIVE RELATIVE CLAUSE

We have a cat *that is a good mouser.*
restrictive relative clause

A restrictive relative clause is the same as a defining adjective clause. It is essential for the meaning of the sentence. When you leave it out, the sentence has a different meaning. **See also *clause, main clause, adjective clause,* and the Defining and Non-Defining Adjective Clause chart in the Appendix.**

RUN-ON SENTENCE

The airplanes whined overhead they were dropping leaflets.

A run-on sentence is two sentences put together without any conjunction, subordinator, or punctuation. Run-on sentences are not typically used in formal writing. **See also *sentence.***

> **Compare**
> The airplanes whined overhead; they were dropping leaflets.
>
> The airplanes whined overhead while they were dropping leaflets.

SECOND PERSON

You should take Spanish next year.

Is this *your* book?

Personal and possessive pronouns have person. Second person shows who is being spoken to. **See *pronoun, personal pronoun,* and *person.***

SENTENCE

A single apple / **fell from the tree.**
    subject   predicate

The black and tan dog / **howled at the sirens.**
    subject   predicate

A sentence has a subject and a predicate. It must have both. **See also *subject* and *predicate.***

SENTENCE FRAGMENT

A single apple from the tree. | There is no predicate because there is no verb.

Falling down. | A word group without a subject or predicate.

A single apple fell. On my head. | Sometimes a period breaks a sentence into fragments.

A single apple fell. Because the wind blew it down.

A sentence fragment is often an incomplete sentence because the end punctuation was incorrectly done. Sometimes a period, question mark, or exclamation mark breaks a sentence into fragments.

SIMPLE SENTENCE

A single apple fell from the tree.

The boys ordered four pizzas with pepperoni, sausage, black olive, and green chile.

A simple sentence has one clause. **See *clause* and *sentence*.**

SINGULAR

Sheila ate an *orange.*   *He* has to get up early.
singular noun   singular noun   singular pronoun

Singular means the noun or pronoun shows only one. **See also *plural*.**

SPLIT INFINITIVE

"*To* boldly *go* where no man has gone before," is said at the beginning of each Star Trek episode.

A split infinitive has one or more words inserted between the *to* and the base form of the verb. **See also *base form*, *verb*, and *verbal*.**

STATE OF BEING VERB

Rita *was* a school teacher. I *am* a handsome man.
noun phrase   adjective phrase

The oak tree *is* in the pasture.
adverbial prepostional phrase

The State of Being Verb is simply *Be* used as a copula or linking verb. It connects a subject to a word or words describing (adjectives), identifying (nouns), or telling the location of (adverbial prepositional phrases) the subject. *Be* is one of the stative verbs, which show unchanging conditions.

STATIVE VERB

Stative verbs in English have several categories.

I *see* a monkey in the tree.
sensory perception

Petunia *has* a new hat.
relationship

Chiang *believes* the story.
mental perception

The bat *weighs* one pound.
measurement

She *dislikes* that movie.
emotion

The roof *is* hot.
state

We *understood* the problem.
stative verb

I *am seeing* better now.
progressive verb

You can use a verb as a stative verb in some instances and as a progressive verb in another. Some stative verbs are *believe, have, belong, contain, cost, differ,* and *own. That, who, where, until,* and *if* are some of the subordinators.

Any verb stating an unchanging condition or state is a stative verb. **See also *Predicate Adjective, Predicate Noun,* and *Phrases.***

SUBJECT/COMPLETE SUBJECT

The boy is running.
noun as the subject

I am going shopping.
pronoun as the subject

The rolling green hills of Kentucky are a beautiful sight.
noun phrase as the subject

The subject generally comes before the predicate and usually is the topic of the sentence. The subject is a noun, a pronoun, noun phrase, or a noun clause. **See also *noun, pronoun, noun phrase, noun clause,* and *predicate.***

SUBJECT-VERB AGREEMENT

The Cocker Spaniel **jumps** for joy.

singular subject   singular verb

The children **play** at the park.

plural subject   plural verb

The subject and verb must agree in number. English has the remnants of an older verb system. In this system, the verb took a different ending for each person. See *Person.* Today, the only change is for third person singular. This includes the pronouns *he, she,* and *it.* These verbs take an "s" ending. See *pronouns.* **See also** *subject, verb, singular,* **and** *plural.*

SUBORDINATE CLAUSE/DEPENDENT CLAUSE

My mother knew *that I would be home by curfew.*

> The subordinate clause is a noun clause.

My daughter, *who has several children of her own,* still works full time.

> The subordinate clause is an adjective clause.

My mother lives in Arkansas where she was born.

> The subordinate clause is an adverbial clause.

A subordinate clause gives information about the main clause. It has a subject and a predicate, but it does not have much meaning without the main clause. It's meaning is dependent on the main clause. It may be a noun clause, an adjective clause, or an adverbial clause. **See also** *main clause, subject, predicate, noun clause, adjective clause,* **and** *adverbial clause.*

Subjunctive Mood

If I *were* a sparrow, I *would* fly away.

You *should eat* something now.

The form of a verb shows its mode or mood. Mode or mood tells the writer's or speaker's attitude about the statement. English has three moods. A verb in the subjunctive mood suggests, wishes, recommends, requires or guesses. A verb in the subjunctive mood may change its form, or it may take a modal auxiliary verb. **See also *verb* and *modal auxiliary verb.***

Subordination

It began to rain *while we were fishing.*

Give this to the boy *who has a cute smile!*

That, who, where, until and *if* are some of the subordinators.

Subordination is the joining of a subordinate or dependent clause to a main or independent clause. **See also *clause, subordinate clause* or *dependent clause,* and *main* or *independent clause.***

Subordinator/Subordinating Conjunction

The jacuzzi *that* we bought is still not installed.

The grocery store *where* I buy my fresh produce just went out of business.

My son, *who* just celebrated his 21st birthday, is going

to Europe.

We biked *until* we were exhausted.

If my dad comes soon, we can catch a ride to the movies.

A subordinator joins a subordinate clause to a main clause. While some grammars call these subordinating conjunctions, they are not true conjunctions. They do more than just join two clauses: They also tell the relationship between the two clauses. **See also *subordinate clause, main clause,* and *conjunction.***

SUPERLATIVE

That is the *smallest* orange I have ever seen.
<small>superlative</small>

Matilda is the *prettiest* girl in school.
<small>superlative</small>

This is the *most* spaghetti I have ever eaten.
<small>superlative</small>

The superlative is a form of the adjective. Superlative shows the most or least of a group of the same thing. You make the superlative by adding *-est* or using *least, worst, most* or *best.* **See also *adjectives.***

TENSE

I *run* every day.
present tense

I *ran* yesterday.
past tense

I *will run* tomorrow.
future tense

Tense relates the action of the verb and the time of the event it describes. Tense shows the time of the action. There are three basic tenses: present, past, and future. There are also the progressive and perfect tenses. **See also** *perfect tense, progressive tense,* **and** *verb.*

THIRD PERSON

He plays on the soccer team.

She went to *their* house for dinner.

They went to the movies on Friday.

Personal and possessive pronouns have person. Third person shows who is being spoken about. *See pronoun, personal pronoun, person, first person, second person* **and** *person.*

TRANSITIVE VERBS

Carl *hit* the ball.
transitive verb

> The subject is *Carl.*
> The direct object is *the ball.*

Karla *caught* a high fly ball.
transitive verb

> The subject is *Karla.*
> The direct object is *a high fly ball*

Amy *thought* we were here.
transitive verb

> The subject is *Carol.*
> The direct object is *that we were at the park*

A transitive verb transfers or carries the action from the subject to an object. You can tell the verb is transitive when you find a direct object. **See also *verb, direct object, subject,* and the Irregular Verbs chart in the Appendix.**

VERB

Jeremy *runs* down the hill.
verb

> In this sentence, the verb shows an action.

Bones *contain* calcium.
verb

> In this sentence, the verb shows a state.

James and Matthew *are* intelligent.
verb

> In this sentence, the verb links the subject to a predicate adjective.

A verb appears in the predicate of a sentence. It tells an action or a state. It also may link the subject to a predicate adjective or predicate noun. **See also *linking verb, action verb, stative verb, subject, predicate, predicate adjective,* and *predicate noun.***

VERB CONJUGATION

I *jog* before breakfast everyday.

He *jogs* after dinner.

He *was* a champion prize fighter.

They *were* his biggest fans.

I *jog* everyday.

I *jogged* yesterday.

Verb conjugation is the changes in the verb forms to show person, number, tense, and mood. **See also *verb, person, number, tense,* and *mood.***

> Verbs change form to show person.
>
> Verbs change form to show number.
>
> Verbs change form to show tense.

VERB GROUP

We *have eaten* already.   We *may go* to the movies later.

verb group   verb group

Do you always *run* every day?

Verb   group

A verb group has a verb plus an auxiliary verb. Some grammars call this a verb phrase. **See also *verb, auxiliary verb,* and *phrase.***

VERBAL/VERBAL NOUN (GERUNDS AND INFINITIVES)

Swimming is an aerobic activity.

gerund or verbal noun

I like *swimming* in the afternoons.

gerund or verbal noun

> Gerunds are the present participle used as a noun.
>
> Infinitives are the base form of a verb plus *to*.

To write is my life.

infinitive or verbal noun

I live *to write.*

infinitive or verbal noun

A verbal noun is a form of a verb. You use it as a noun. There are two kinds of verbal nouns, gerunds and infinitives. **See also *verb, participle,* and *noun.***

VERBAL PHRASE

I love *to bike through the hills.*
verbal phrase

> In this sentence, *biking through the hills* is a participle phrase.

Biking through the hills, we always get a good workout.
verbal phrase

> In this sentence, *to bike through the hills* is an infinitive phrase.

A verbal phrase is a verbal plus any objects, modifiers, or both. A verbal phrase can be a participle phrase, infinitive phrase, or a noun phrase. **See also *objects, modifiers, participle phrase, noun phrase,* and *phrase.***

VERB PHRASE

The bride *caught her long white train* on *a nail.*

He *jumped up.*

> In some grammars a verb phrase is only the verb plus an adverb.

A phrase is a group of words functioning as a unit. A verb phrase has a verb, its objects, its modifiers, or both. Another name for a verb phrase is *predicate.*

VOICE

Joe *hit* the ball.

Nick *ate* the cake.

The ball *was hit by* Joe.

The cake *was eaten by* Nick.

> In active voice, the subject acts. The action moves from the subject to the direct object.
>
> In passive voice, the subject is acted upon. In passive voice, the action moves back to the subject.

Voice indicates whether the subject acts or is acted upon. Only transitive verbs can make a change in voice. **See also *subject, transitive verb,* and *direct object.***

WH-QUESTION

Why are we having spaghetti tonight?

A question is a kind of sentence. This sentence addresses the listener or reader and asks for an expression of fact, opinion, or belief. You can use a question word like *what, when, where,* and *why* to form a question. You put a question mark at the end of a question. **See also *interrogative pronoun, question,* and *sentence.***

YES-NO QUESTION

Can we have spaghetti tonight?

A question is a kind of sentence. This sentence addresses the listener or reader and asks for an expression of fact, opinion, or belief. A yes-no question only requires a yes or no answer. You put a question mark at the end of a question. **See also *sentence* and *question.***

APPENDIX

CONJUNCTIVE ADVERBS

FUNCTION	CONJUNCTIVE ADVERB
Addition	besides, furthermore, moreover, in addition
Likeness	likewise, similarly, in the same way
Contrast	however, nevertheless, still, nonetheless, conversely, otherwise, instead, in contrast, on the other hand
Cause and effect	accordingly, consequently, hence, therefore, as a result, for this reason
A means-and-an end	thus, thereby, by this means, in this manner
Reinforcement	for example, for instance, in fact, in particular, indeed
Time	meanwhile, then, subsequently, afterward, earlier, later

DEFINING ADJECTIVE CLAUSES/
RESTRICTIVE RELATIVE CLAUSES

I want a shoe *that fits*.

The man *who ordered the pepperoni pizza* is my father.

The bird *that ate the worm* is a Robin.

Take this drink to the woman *who is wearing a pink dress*.

Mr. Botone bought the car *that had the lowest price*.

The car *that had the lowest price* was a red convertible.

The women from our neighborhood love to dance with men *who dance the tango*.

Children *who eat lots of sugar* often have many cavities.

The cowboy tried to rope the steer *that had the longest tail*.

Non-defining Adjective Clauses/
Non-restrictive Relative Clauses

I want new shoes, *which I hope to buy soon.*

My father, *who ordered the pepperoni pizza,* is also our coach.

That Robin ate a worm, *which is one of its favorite foods.*

Take this drink to Ms. Cheng, *who is wearing a pink dress.*

Mr. Botone, *who bought the car with the lowest price,* is Director of the Indian Center.

The red convertible, *which had the lowest price,* is a gift for his son's graduation.

My favorite dance partner is Mr. Gonzalez, *who loves to dance the tango.*

Alfred, *who eats lots of sugar,* has many cavities.

Buddy, *who is a cowboy,* tried to rope the steer with the longest tail.

IRREGULAR VERBS

BASE FORM	PAST TENSE	PAST PARTICIPLE
arise	arose	arisen
awake	awoke	awakened
be	was, were	been
bear	bore	borne, born
begin	began	begun
bend	bent	bent
bid	bade, bid	bidden, bid
bind	bound	bound
bite	bit	bitten
bleed	bled	bled
blow	blew	blown
break	broke	broken
breed	bred	bred
bring	brought	brought
burst	burst	burst
buy	bought	bought
cast	cast	cast
catch	caught	caught

IRREGULAR VERBS

BASE FORM	PAST TENSE	PAST PARTICIPLE
choose	chose	chosen
cling	clung	clung
come	came	come
cost	cost	cost
creep	crept	crept
cut	cut	cut
deal	dealt	dealt
dig	dug	dug
do	did	done
draw	drew	drawn
dream	dreamed, dreamt	dreamed, dreamt
drink	drank	drunk
drive	drove	driven
eat	ate	eaten
fall	fell	fallen
feed	fed	fed
feel	felt	felt
fight	fought	fought

IRREGULAR VERBS

BASE FORM	PAST TENSE	PAST PARTICIPLE
find	found	found
flee	fled	fled
fling	flung	flung
fly	flew	flown
forget	forgot	forgotten
forgive	forgave	forgiven
freeze	froze	frozen
get	got	gotten
give	gave	given
go	went	gone
grow	grew	grown
hang	hung, hanged	hung, hanged
have	had	had
hear	heard	heard
hide	hid	hidden
hold	held	held
keep	kept	kept
kneel	knelt	knelt

IRREGULAR VERBS

BASE FORM	PAST TENSE	PAST PARTICIPLE
know	knew	known
lead	led	led
leave	left	left
lend	lent	lent
lie	lay	lain
light	lit, lighted	lit, lighted
lose	lost	lost
make	made	made
mean	meant	meant
put	put	put
read	read	read
ride	rode	ridden
ring	rang	rung
rise	rose	risen
say	said	said
see	saw	seen
sell	sold	sold
send	sent	sent

IRREGULAR VERBS

BASE FORM	PAST TENSE	PAST PARTICIPLE
set	set	set
shake	shook	shaken
shine	shone, shined	shone, shined
shoot	shot	shot
shrink	shrank, shrunk	shrunk, shrunken
sing	sang	sung
sink	sank	sunk, sunken
sit	sat	sat
sleep	slept	leapt
speak	spoke	spoken
spend	spent	spent
spin	spun	spun
spit	spat	spat
spread	spread	spread
spring	sprang, sprung	sprung
stand	stood	stood
steal	stole	stolen
stick	stuck	stuck

IRREGULAR VERBS

BASE FORM	PAST TENSE	PAST PARTICIPLE
sting	stunk, stank	stunk
strike	struck	struck, stricken
string	strung	strung
sweep	swept	swept
swim	swam, swum	swum
swing	swung, swang	swung
take	took	taken
teach	taught	taught
tear	tore	torn
think	thought	thought
wake	woke, waked	waked, woken
wear	wore	worn

MODAL AUXILIARIES

VERB	USE
can	*capability:* You *can* do it. *permission: Can* she do it now?
could	*object of a wish (ability):* We wish that we *could* go. *a condition:* If they *could* finish early, they would be happy. *A distinct possibility:* A rainstorm *could* arrive by midnight.
may	a mild possibility: Our new boss *may* be a woman. permission: *May* we go now?
might	*a remote possibility:* They *might* get here on time. *the result of a contrary-to-fact condition:* If they had arrived on time, we *might* have gone to dinner.
must	*an absolute obligation:* You *must* have insurance to drive. *a firm conclusion:* She *must* be a great dancer.
ought	*strong recommendation:* They *ought* to stop. likelihood: They *ought* to win tonight.
should	*advice:* You *should* take an umbrella today. *expectation:* Grandmother *should* be here soon.
would	*the result of a condition or event:* If I were a millionaire, I *would* buy a new house. *the object of a wish (willingness):* I wish that you *would* sing with us.

PREPOSITIONS

Prepositions normally show a relatiionhip between nouns, pronouns, and verbals to other words in the sentence. The following charts show the most common meanings for some of these relationships.

MOST COMMON PREPOSITIONS

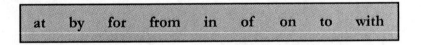

at	by	for	from	in	of	on	to	with

AT

Space

1. Point or intersect	meet *at* the corner
2. target	Throw the ball *at* the picture.
3. general area	Meet me *at* the library.

Time

We met *at* 3:00.
I dream *at* night.

Degree

Water boils *at* 100° C.

Other

He works *at* staying on his diet.
She is good *at* baking.

MOST COMMON PREPOSITIONS (continued)

BY

Space

1. Nearness   the desk *by* the wall

2. Past   drove *by* the school

3. Measure   That room is 12 *by* 10 feet.

Time

1. No later than   Be *home by* 3 p.m.

2. During   We travel *by* day.

3. after   day *by* day

Degree

1. Reduplication   little *by* little, inch *by* inch
   (gradual increase)

2. Degree of failure   You won *by* a mile
   or success   You missed the bus *by* ten
                         minutes.

Other

Agency or action   I can do this *by* myself.
                     We went *by* the back road.
                     By his own confession, he did it.

MOST COMMON PREPOSITIONS (continued)

FOR

Space

1. Goal	We set out *for* Boston.
2. Distance	We walked *for* five miles.
3. Exchange or paired	Use margarine *for* butter. She mistook him *for* the mayor.
4. Being	one bad apple *for* every good one

Time

Duration	We stayed *for* three months.

Degree

1. Exchangeor amount	sell *for* $2
2. extent	The construction goes *for* 2 miles.

Other

1. Reason	New Mexico is famous *for* its Indians.
2. Purpose	We fished *for* bass.
3. Have or find	We trained *for* the track team.
4. Effect	Exercise is good *for* you.

MOST COMMON PREPOSITIONS (continued)

FROM

Space

1. Starting point	He traveled *from* Boston to Maine.
2. Origin	A woman *from* Chicago
3. Out of	I took a cup *from* the cabinet.

Time

Starting point	I work *from* 9:00 a.m. to 5:00 p.m.

Degree

from 40° to 50°
from 1 to 2 dollars

Other

1. Source	Perfume is made *from* natural scents.
2. Cause	The flower is wet *from* the dew.
3. Negative action	We want to keep her *from* making a mistake. know right *from* wrong

MOST COMMON PREPOSITIONS (continued)

IN

Space

1. Enclosure	The clothes are *in* the closet.
2. Effecting an area	He got hit *in* the head.

Time

1. Certain time	WWII ended *in* 1945.
2. Before a certain time	be ready *in* ten minutes

Other

1. Condition	said *in* anger
	in trouble
	paid *in* cash
2. reference	latest *in* fashion
	in my opinion

MOST COMMON PREPOSITIONS (CONTINUED)

OF

Space

1. Belonging to

the city *of* Detroit
the state *of* Texas
the University *of* Arkansas

2. Distance

a mile north *of* here

Time

1. Before

a quarter *of* one

2. During

of recent times

Degree

Part

one *of* the team
give *of* one's time

Other

1. Possession

a friend *of* mine
a person *of* honor

2. Property

a cabinet made *of* hard wood

3. Origin or source

William *of* Orange

4. Cause

died *of* old age

MOST COMMON PREPOSITIONS (CONTINUED)

ON

Space

1. Contact	*on* the wall
2. Along	*on* the avenue
3. Day, date, occasion, or moment	*on* Sunday *on* her fifth birthday

Time

Action	He threw his coat *on* the desk.

Degree

Receiving the action	The spotlight fell *on* the actor.

Other

1. Source	living *on* bread and water
2. Condition	*on* leave *on* fire *on* business *on* a plane
3. About	a book *on* Asian history
4. Possession	not a penny *on* me

MOST COMMON PREPOSITIONS (CONTINUED)

To

Space

   1. Direction   go *to* the mall
                             Come to my house.

Time

   1. Until   Hours: 9:00 a.m. *to* 5:00 pm

   2. Before   fifteen minutes *to* eleven

Degree

   Part   two pints *to* the quart

Other

   1. Condition   rotten *to* the core
                             starved *to* death
                             rise *to* power

   2. Relation   pinned *to* her dress
                             worked *to* that end
                             deaf *to* her cries
                             parallel *to* the road

MOST COMMON PREPOSITIONS (CONTINUED)

WITH

Space

1. Alongside or near — even *with* the wall
   walk *with* me

2. Direction — bend *with* the wind

3. Share space — Mix the roses *with* the daisies.

Time

1. Same time — rises *with* the sun

2. During — grow older *with* time
   All things fade *with* time

Degree

1. Proportion — grow better *with* age

2. Comparison — one day *with* another

Other

1. Property or belonging — *with* skill
   to be *with* me
   a dress identical *with* theone I
   already have

2. Result — trembling *with* fear

3. Together — cheeseburger with fries

4. Against — wrestling *with* my problems

SENTENCE TYPES

TYPE	EXAMPLE
Declarative sentences state something.	My dog has fleas. My bird loves geraniums. Apples grow on trees.
Exclamatory sentences begin with what and how.	How beautiful the mountains are today! What a lovely day!
Imperative sentences command.	Stand up straight! Come to the table. Please hand me that book. Move the table over there.
Interrogative sentences ask a question.	How much is that doggie in the window? What kind of candy do you like? Will you be coming to the party? Where is my book. Do you ever think of him?

SOME SUBORDINATORS

TYPE	SUBORDINATORS	EXAMPLE
Condition	if, unless	You cannot go to the movies *unless* you finish your homework.
Cause	because, since, as, inasmuch as, forasmuch as	*Since* he's been gone, she's been sad. *Inasmuch as* we are rich, we should buy a new house.
Purpose	so that, lest, in order that	You will be late *lest* you leave now.
Result or Effect	so that	Take your vitamins *so that* you stay healthy.
Concession	though, although, even if, even though,	*Even though* you are right, I still disagree. *Although* she misses him, she remains busy with her life.
Relative Pronouns	who, that, which, whose whoever, whichever	The book, *which* I left on the table, is gone. Take *whichever* one you want.

SUGGESTED READING

Biber, D. (1988). *Variation across speech and writing.* Cambridge: Cambridge University Press.

Celcia-Murcia, M. & Larsen-Freeman, D. (1983). *The grammar book: an ESL/EFL teachers course.* Cambridge, MA: Newbury House Publishers.

Chomsky, N. (1957). *Syntactic structures.* The Hague: Mouton.

Chomsky, N. (1965). *Aspects of the theory of syntax.* Cambridge, MA: MIT Press.

Ehrman, M. (1972). *The meanings of the modals in present-day American English.* The Hague: Mouton.

Finegan, E. (1980). *Attitudes toward English usage: the history of a war of words.* New York: Teachers College Press.

Halliday, M. & Hasan, R. (1976). *Cohesion in English.* London: Longman.

Schriffrin, D. (1981). Tense variation in narrative. *Language* 57, pp. 45-62.

Sebeok, T. Ed. (1960). *Style of Language.* Cambridge, MA: MIT Press.

Shopen, T. (1985). *Language typology and syntactic description.* Vol. 2: *Complex constructions.* Cambridge: Cambridge University Press.

Tottie, G. (1982). Where do negative sentences come